CREATED FOR

....

WITH LOVE FROM

....

LOVE
LETTERS

To My Baby

REVISED AND UPDATED EDITION

*A Guided Journal for
Expectant and New Mothers*

VICKEY BANKS

Who ran to help me when I fell,
And would some pretty story tell,
Or kiss the place to make it well?
My mother.

—ANN TAYLOR
"My Mother"

Dear Mom,

CONGRATULATIONS! An awesome miracle has taken place inside your body. I've read books on it and experienced it twice, yet I am still totally confounded by how God makes babies. A heart that pumps blood, eyelids that open and close, fingers and toes that wiggle and delight—how can these masterpieces be minutely formed inside your increasingly cramped tummy?

Whether you are a first-time mother or like the woman in the shoe—with so many children she didn't know what to do!—this book is for you. Pregnancy and motherhood are so astounding that your heart simply won't be big enough to hold all the wonder and dreams your new baby will evoke. This guided journal was designed to help you capture them all in a very special collection of love letters and prayers—to be given one day to the precious child who inspired them.

Since this is yours and your baby's journey to record, feel free to adapt any of the prompts to write about what you most want to communicate. Furthermore, since your baby might be a boy or girl (or even twins or triplets!), I will alternate the use of "she" and "he" throughout the devotions.

And now, pick up a pen and write about your love on paper. May God use your words to write your love upon your little one's heart forever.

With love, *Vickey*

Dear Heavenly Father,

As I begin recording letters and prayers in this book, I pray

....

....

....

....

....

....

....

May the favor of the Lord our God rest on us;
establish the work of our hands for us—
yes, establish the work of our hands.

—PSALM 90:17

Announcing!

Place ultrasound photo or baby announcement here

This Is the Miracle

Before you were conceived
I wanted you.
Before you were born
I loved you.
Before you were here an hour
I would die for you.
This is the miracle of love.

—MAUREEN HAWKINS

The Most Wonderful

NEWS

You Are Coming!

photo

At that time Mary got ready and hurried to a town in the hill country of Judah, where she entered Zechariah's home and greeted Elizabeth.

—LUKE 1:39–40

The young virgin, Mary, had just been told the most amazing news: She was pregnant! And the bearer of these tidings wasn't her doctor or even an ancient do-it-yourself home pregnancy test. God had sent His trusted confidante, the angel Gabriel, to deliver this sensational secret. Luke tells us that immediately Mary threw together some things and raced to see her cousin Elizabeth. She simply couldn't wait to tell someone her good news!

Your own pregnancy may not have been heralded by an angel, but the discovery that Baby was on the way was a miracle just the same. Who did you run to with your incredible announcement? Did you give them clever clues or just blurt it out with abandon? Take time to tell Baby about the moment you knew he was on the way and how you went about sharing the wonderful surprise with family and friends.

Dearest Miracle of Mine,

I knew I was pregnant when

At first I felt

Your coming is good news because

The first person I told was

I also couldn't wait to tell

To celebrate

Dear Heavenly Father,

Thank You for the wonderful gift of a new baby! As I reflect on this exciting news, I pray

....

....

Moments I want to remember from this time:

-

-

The whole earth is filled with awe at your wonders;
where morning dawns, where evening fades,
you call forth songs of joy.

— PSALM 65:8

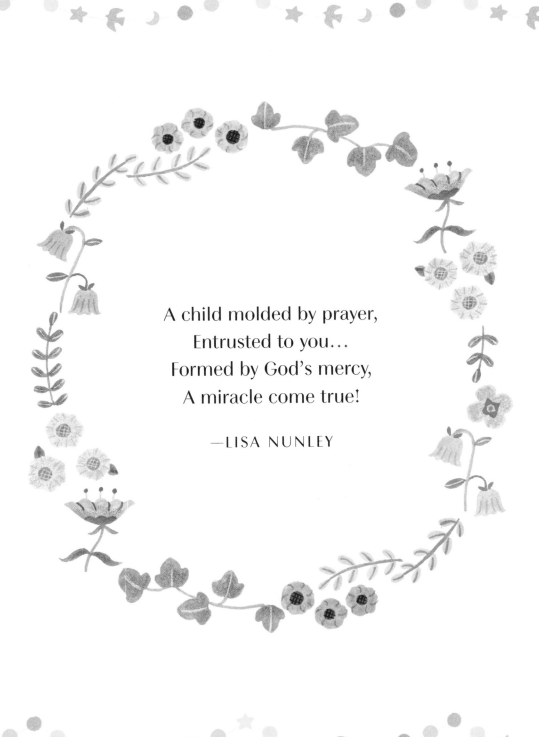

A child molded by prayer,
Entrusted to you…
Formed by God's mercy,
A miracle come true!

—LISA NUNLEY

Handmade by

GOD

The Miracle of You

photo

You made all the delicate, inner
parts of my body
and knit me together
in my mother's womb.

—PSALM 139:13 (NLT)

Just imagine . . . the Creator of the entire universe, the One who made the heavens and the earth, the originator of all things living, is personally creating your unborn child. That's right. The same God who hangs the stars in the night skies and balances the clouds is at work this very moment on His latest masterpiece—your precious baby! He is weaving together all her teeny, tiny, intricate parts. He hears every beat of her heart. He has already felt the brush of her eyelashes. He has put her hairs in place and knows where her ticklish spots are. Your baby is being handmade by God.

When He knits, God doesn't make mistakes. He neither misses nor adds an extra stitch. Before your baby can even do or say anything on her own, she is a perfect, one-of-a-kind original. She bears God's brand name and has incomparable value because of her Creator. Nothing can ever diminish her worth. Tell Baby how special you think she is and what knowing she is being handmade by God means to you.

Dearest Little Masterpiece,

When I picture you being formed inside my womb ....

....

....

....

Knowing God is forming you makes me feel ....

....

....

....

I want you to know how valuable you are, because ....

....

....

....

God hears your heartbeat, and I ....

....

....

....

You will always be special to me, because ....

....

....

....

I'm so grateful that ....

....

....

....

Dear Heavenly Father,

Thank You for forming my precious baby.
My prayer today is that

....

....

Moments I want to remember from this time:

-

-

For we are God's handiwork, created in
Christ Jesus to do good works, which God
prepared in advance for us to do.

—EPHESIANS 2:10

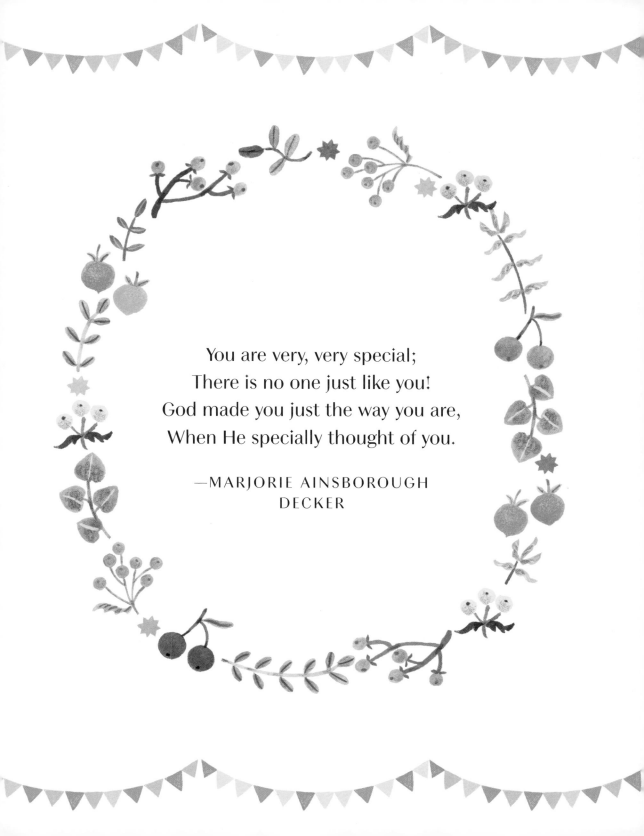

You are very, very special;
There is no one just like you!
God made you just the way you are,
When He specially thought of you.

—MARJORIE AINSBOROUGH
DECKER

Signs of
LIFE

Making Your Presence Known

photo

As soon as the sound of your greeting reached my ears, the baby in my womb leaped for joy.

—LUKE 1:44

After many years of being barren, Elizabeth was miraculously pregnant. When her cousin Mary visited, Elizabeth's baby literally leapt in her womb. Can't you see her soothing hands immediately moving to caress her ample abdomen? Can you picture the look of sheer delight on her face? You've probably done the same thing when your little wonder began to twist and turn. Isn't it the most incredible feeling? Life. Inside yours. Simply indescribable!

What signs of life have you experienced from the baby within you? Have you heard his rapidly beating heart or stared in total amazement (quite possibly with tears running down your face) at his image on an ultrasound screen? Or maybe you've been overcome by feelings not nearly as sentimental, with morning sickness holding you hostage. Have you grimaced in discomfort as a determined foot seemed destined to poke its way out of your body? Elizabeth's unborn baby responded to the sound of Mary's voice. What sounds and smells does your wee one respond to? Ah, the signs of life. Someone special is making his presence known!

Dearest Life Within,

When I first heard your heartbeat, I

Seeing you move on the ultrasound screen was

I first felt you move

Feeling you inside me is

You are most active when

During my pregnancy, I felt

Dear Heavenly Father,

As my baby begins to grow and move inside me

....

....

Moments I want to remember from this time:

-

-

My frame was not hidden from you
when I was made in the secret place,
when I was woven together in the depths of the earth.
Your eyes saw my unformed body;
all the days ordained for me were written in your book
before one of them came to be.

—PSALM 139:15–16

Jack be nimble, Jack be quick,
Jack jumped over the candlestick.

Showers of
LOVE

Preparing for You

photo

*Sarah said, "God has brought me
laughter, and everyone who hears
about this will laugh with me."*

—GENESIS 21:6

Sarah had waited a long time to have a baby.
Genesis 18:11 says, "Abraham and Sarah were
already old and well advanced in years, and Sarah
was past the age of childbearing." Abraham was
one hundred years old and Sarah was ninety—
not the average age for first-time parents! Bible
commentator Matthew Henry minces no words on
this subject when he says they "both were old and
as good as dead." However, God brought laughter
into their lives with the birth of sweet baby Isaac.
Clearly, this was cause for celebration! Sarah was
sure everyone who heard her good news would
laugh with joy.

Can you just imagine the parties and preparations
Isaac's long-awaited birth brought? Blue blankies
and booties must have appeared from everywhere!
Surely there was a treasured heirloom or two
passed down to this child of promise. Who has
been celebrating the promise of your baby with
you? How have you readied your home to welcome
your newest family member? May the sounds of
laughter reach your listening little one as her arrival
is celebrated.

Special Gifts	Givers
_____	_____
_____	_____
_____	_____
_____	_____
_____	_____
_____	_____
_____	_____
_____	_____
_____	_____
_____	_____

A party for me? thought Pooh
to himself. How grand!

—A.A. MILNE, *Christopher Robin*
Gives a Pooh Party

Dearest Cause for Laughter,

Friends have shared their joy by ....

....

....

....

Celebrations have included ....

....

....

....

Daddy and I have appreciated the love and support of ....

....

....

....

To prepare for your coming ....

....

....

....

To decorate your room ....

....

....

....

Special things you have inherited include ....

....

....

....

Special Messages and Showers of Love

Save these pages to record special words of welcome to your baby from loved ones. You can either copy the notes yourself from cards or messages, or invite friends and family to pen a sweet note in their own handwriting.

POSTCARD

POSTCARD

There will be showers of blessing.

–EZEKIEL 34:26

Dear Heavenly Father,

Thank You for all the friends and family who are excited for Baby's arrival. I pray

....

....

Moments I want to remember from this time:

-

-

They broke bread in their homes and ate
together with glad and sincere hearts.

—ACTS 2:46

Babies bring joy to our
hearts and laughter
to our homes.

—RAE WAKELIN

Waiting and
WONDERING

Anticipating Your Arrival

photo

Hope deferred makes the heart sick,
but a longing fulfilled is a tree of life.

—PROVERBS 13:12

Eve was the first pregnant woman—the first in line to wait. Can you just imagine? Her stomach began to bulge, and she felt something move inside her. She must have wondered what was happening to her body. God had warned her that she would have great pains in child-bearing. But how bad must pain get for God to consider it great? Eve had never even seen a human child. What would it look like? Would it be a boy or a girl? How in the world was it going to come out? The waiting and wondering must have seemed endless.

Does it seem like you have been waiting an eternity for Baby to arrive? Do you feel your hope is being deferred? One thing is certain, you will not be pregnant forever. Delivery day will come! What thoughts dance about in your head as you wait for Baby? Soon your longing will be fulfilled. Hang in there. New life is coming!

Dearest One I Wait For,

When it comes to waiting

I keep wondering

I imagine you will look like

When I dream about you,

In the future, I hope you will

Mommy is getting restless because

Dear Heavenly Father,

Waiting is so hard, but I pray

....

....

Moments I want to remember from this time:

*

*

But those who hope in the Lord
will renew their strength.
They will soar on wings like eagles;
they will run and not grow weary,
they will walk and not be faint.

—ISAIAH 40:31

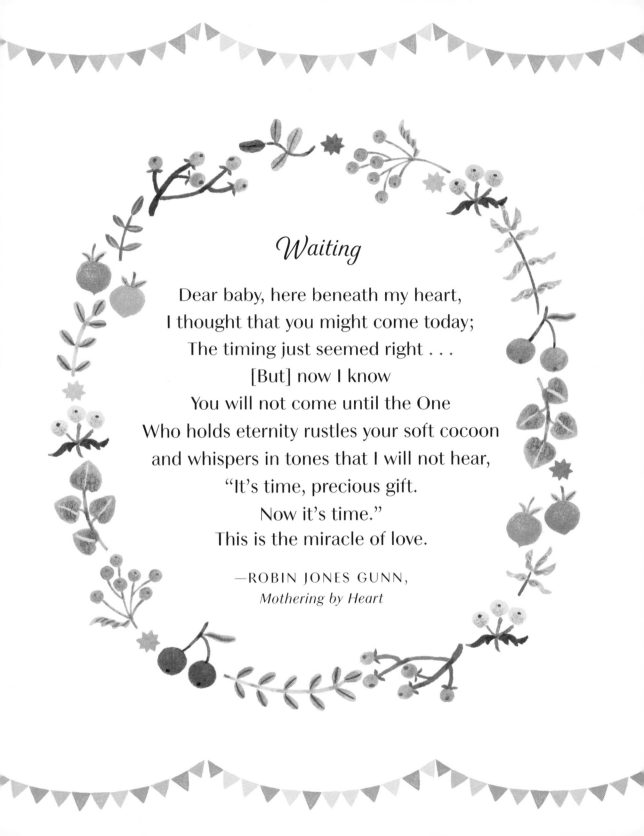

Waiting

Dear baby, here beneath my heart,
I thought that you might come today;
The timing just seemed right . . .
[But] now I know
You will not come until the One
Who holds eternity rustles your soft cocoon
and whispers in tones that I will not hear,
"It's time, precious gift.
Now it's time."
This is the miracle of love.

—ROBIN JONES GUNN,
Mothering by Heart

Opening
CEREMONIES

Delivery Day!

photo

From birth I have relied on you;
you brought me forth from my mother's womb.
I will ever praise you.

—PSALM 71:6

Oh, miracle of miracles! Can you believe the day is finally here? Not since Moses led the enslaved Hebrews out of Egypt has there been such cheering! So, break out the noisemakers; the umbilical cord has been cut, and it's time for the opening ceremonies of God's latest creation. Your baby has been brought forth! That bundle of joy you hold in your arms was just yesterday curled inside your crowded womb. God has done the inconceivable. He has brought forth life! This is a day worth remembering. A day worth recording.

What do you most want to tell the one who will someday call you Mommy? What do you want to forever write upon that precious little one's heart? Think over the sights, sounds, excitement, and emotions of this never-to-be-duplicated day. Your heart is no doubt overflowing with sentiments. When you have time to breathe amid all the excitement of your baby's arrival, take a few moments to capture the feeling of this very special event.

Birth Certificate

WELCOME HOME!

Announcing _____

Born _____ Time _____

Weighing _____ lbs. _____ oz.

Measuring _____

Hair _____ Eyes _____

Proud Parents Are _____

_____

YOU'VE ARRIVED!

Attach hospital bracelet or baby photos here

Dearest _____ ,
child's name

When I first saw you ....

....

....

....

Holding you in my arms feels ....

....

....

....

Daddy's first words were ....

....

....

....

We chose your name because ....

....

....

....

The thoughts of those waiting to meet you today were ....

....

....

....

Of all the emotions of the day, I mostly felt ....

....

....

....

Dear Heavenly Father,

Thank You for

....

....

Moments I want to remember from this time:

-

-

For you make me glad by your deeds, Lord;
I sing for joy at what your hands have done.

—PSALM 92:4

Lost in Wonder

Once in a while.
I'm lost in the wonder
Of life's greatest joy
As I gaze on the face
Of my wee sleeping boy.

—MILLY WALTON

Home at
LAST

Celebrating Your Coming

photo

And if I go and prepare a place for you,
I will come back and take you to be with
me that you also may be where I am.

—JOHN 14:3

Jesus wanted the disciples to know He was preparing a special place just for them. A place where they could stay with Him forever. A place they could all call home. Just the word sounds warm and inviting, doesn't it? There truly is no place in the world like home. And what a homecoming celebration it must have been when Jesus personally escorted His disciples to their custom-built heavenly haven.

For months, you have been preparing a special place for Baby. You've probably decorated a nursery and set up the baby swing. You've shopped and maybe even sewed in anticipation of this very special day. Your newborn's blankies have been washed and are waiting as warm welcoming gifts. But wait no more! Today is Homecoming Day! What did Baby wear for this all-important occasion? Who has been waiting to love and care for him? Tell Baby all about this very special day, his home, and the family he's being welcomed into.

Dearest Welcomed One,

For your big homecoming, you wore

Waiting to greet you were

Daddy cares for you by

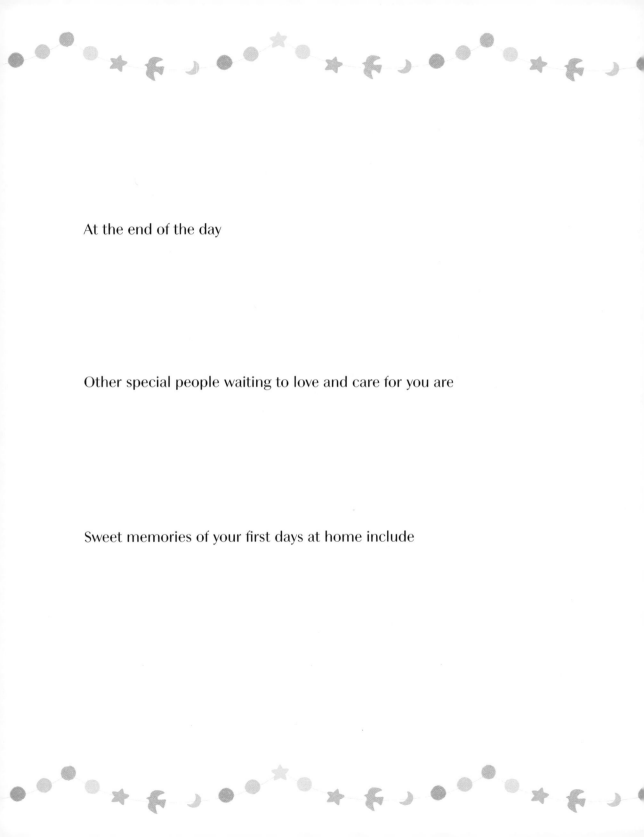

At the end of the day

Other special people waiting to love and care for you are

Sweet memories of your first days at home include

Welcome to the family!

Our Family Tree

father

Name _____
Place of Birth_____
Date of Birth _____

grandfather

Name _____
Place of Birth _____
Date of Birth _____

grandmother

Name _____
Place of Birth _____
Date of Birth _____

great-grandfather

Name _____
Place of Birth _____
Date of Birth _____

great-grandmother

Name _____
Place of Birth _____
Date of Birth _____

great-grandfather

Name _____
Place of Birth _____
Date of Birth _____

great-grandmother

Name _____
Place of Birth _____
Date of Birth _____

baby looks most like _____

mother

Name _____
Place of Birth _____
Date of Birth _____

grandfather

Name _____
Place of Birth _____
Date of Birth _____

grandmother

Name _____
Place of Birth _____
Date of Birth _____

great-grandfather

Name _____
Place of Birth _____
Date of Birth _____

great-grandmother

Name _____
Place of Birth _____
Date of Birth _____

great-grandmother

Name _____
Place of Birth _____
Date of Birth _____

great-grandfather

Name _____
Place of Birth _____
Date of Birth _____

Dear Heavenly Father,

As we welcome home the newest member of the family,

....

....

Moments I want to remember from this time:

-

-

*Whoever welcomes one of these little children
in my name welcomes me; and whoever welcomes me
does not welcome me but the one who sent me.*

—MARK 9:37

Little Lucy Ladybug

Who cares for you each day?
Oh, I have a lovely Someone,
And I'll tell you, if I may
He is the Heavenly Father,
Who made my bath—and bedroom, too;
And kindly watches over me,
And cares for me…and you!

—MARJORIE AINSBOROUGH
DECKER

The Making of a
MOMMY

Becoming Your Mom

photo

Her children arise and call her blessed;
her husband also, and he praises her.

—PROVERBS 31:28

Proverbs 31 is a description of King Lemuel's dream girl for his son. If she had been a real person, she would have been the original Superwoman. She seemed to lead the perfectly balanced life. She cooked, cleaned, shopped, and sewed. She earned money and made wise investments with it. She was quick to help the needy, but never at the expense of caring for her own family. She even dressed well! The description of her can send us mere mortal women cowering at even the hint of personal comparison, but the idea of her can inspire us to rise into the calling God has planned for us.

What kind of mommy do you want to be? Better yet, what kind of mommy does God want you to be? The making of a truly praiseworthy mom doesn't happen overnight. It takes more than dreaming. It takes time in the trenches of real life. It requires selflessness and sacrifice—loss of sleep and lots of help from the Holy Spirit. But the finished product is sure to someday elicit the *oohs* and *aahs* of all those in your house.

Dearest Mommy Maker,

To me, becoming a mom means ....

....

....

....

I think I would feel worthy of praise if ....

....

....

....

I want to be the kind of mother who ....

....

....

....

To celebrate the sweet connection between mom and baby, use this page to trace your own hand, and then add your baby's inside it for a visual time capsule you can treasure for years to come.

Dear Heavenly Father,

As I step into the role of becoming a mom to a new baby, please help me

....

....

Moments I want to remember from this time:

-

-

"My grace is sufficient for you, for my power is made perfect in weakness." Therefore I will boast all the more gladly about my weaknesses, so that Christ's power may rest on me. . . . For when I am weak, then I am strong.

—2 CORINTHIANS 12:9–10

Making the decision
to have a child—it's
momentous.
It is to decide forever to
have your heart go
walking around outside
your body.

—ELIZABETH STONE

Getting to Know
YOU

Early Days with You

photo

But Mary treasured up all these things
and pondered them in her heart.

—LUKE 2:19

Don't you find it amazing that Jesus was once a little child? Can you even begin to imagine being His mother? Talk about weighty responsibilities! Mary kissed His boo-boos and learned the meanings behind His every cry. She knew what made Him giggle and when His diaper needed changing. She, no doubt, taught Him His first nursery rhymes and sang Him to sleep at night. Mary literally held in her hands and rocked the Son of God! And she tried to remember every beautiful moment.

A mother's heart is a treasure chest that holds something far more valuable than gold or riches. Memories make up its priceless contents. What treasures have you safely stored away these last weeks and months? You and Baby have spent quite a bit of time together now. What sights and sounds have you witnessed that you never want to forget? What have you learned about the love gift God has graciously placed in your care? These are treasured times. Let your priceless child know how precious these days have been to you.

Dearest Memory Maker,

You are happiest when

You get cranky if

When you eat or take a bath

Some of your favorite people are

When you sleep

My favorite time with you is

FAMOUS FIRSTS!

Smiled ....
date

Laughed out loud ....
date

Slept through the night ....
date

Rolled over ....
date

Cut a tooth ....
date

Sat alone ....
date

Crawled ....
date

Clapped ....
date

Played peek-a-boo ....
date

Said first word ....
date

Pulled up ....
date

Stood alone ....
date

Took first steps ....
date

Blew first kiss ....
date

Jumped ....
date

Danced ....
date

Waved bye-bye ....
date

Attended a church service ....
date

Said a prayer ....
date

Baptized or dedicated ....
date

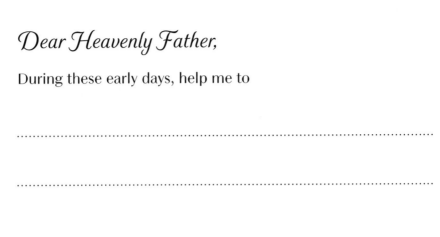

Dear Heavenly Father,

During these early days, help me to

....

....

Moments I want to remember from this time:

-

-

You will keep in perfect peace
those whose minds are steadfast,
because they trust in you.

—ISAIAH 26:3

Cleaning and Scrubbing

Cleaning and Scrubbing
Can wait until tomorrow,
For babies grow up,
We've learned to our sorrow.
So, quiet down cobwebs;
Dust go to sleep;
I'm rocking my baby,
And babies don't keep.

—UNKNOWN

Given to
GOD

Dedicating You to Him

photo

"I prayed for this child, and the Lord has granted me what I asked of him. So now I give him to the LORD. For his whole life he will be given over to the LORD." And he worshiped the LORD there.

—1 SAMUEL 1:27–28

Like so many women, Hannah was desperate to have a child. Scripture says she wept bitterly and wouldn't eat. Perhaps you can identify with the depth of her desire. Hannah chose to pour out her pain in prayer to the only One who could fill her empty arms. When she did, she made God a lofty promise: If He would give her a son, she would in turn dedicate that son to serving God in the temple for his whole life. Hannah was true to her commitment, and her sweet Samuel grew up to be a great man of God.

How might God want you to dedicate your child? What commitments are you willing to make toward Baby's future? Hannah's very life was an example of devotion that her son followed. There is power in example. What will you do to help your child be known for her devotion to God? Tell Baby how you dedicated her, and why you will continue to give her back to God—for her whole life.

Dearest Baby of God,

When I think of your future ....

....

....

....

I am committed to ....

....

....

....

I would like to be a good example of ....

....

....

....

I hope to honor God by..

....

....

....

To dedicate you to God ....

....

....

....

My prayer is that you will honor God by ....

....

....

....

Dear Heavenly Father,

Thank You for entrusting me with Your precious child. I pray that

....

....

Moments I want to remember from this time:

-

-

The Lord bless you
and keep you;
the Lord make his face shine on you
and be gracious to you;
the Lord turn his face toward you
and give you peace.

—NUMBERS 6:24–26

With reverence and devotion,
we dedicate our child to You,
the Lord God Almighty,
Wondrous and Awesome,
Esteemed and Adored.
May this sweet one honor
You all the days of her life.
By grace, You will make
us parents, and from grace,
we pray in Your name.

—ANGELA THOMAS GUFFEY,
Prayers for Expectant Mothers

Everything
CHANGES

The Difference You Make

photo

Listen, I tell you a mystery: We will not all sleep, but we will all be changed.

—1 CORINTHIANS 15:51

It's hard to believe God didn't have newborns in mind when He inspired these words, isn't it? When they are in the house, we certainly don't all sleep, but they definitely need changing! Parenting is a mystery. Just when you think you hold all the clue cards in your hand, you uncover a dilemma you never anticipated. Schedules seem made only to be broken. What works today doesn't always work tomorrow. And what of change? It seems the only constant in this new adventure.

Life will never be the same—and neither will your home—and perhaps your body! Has your house's decorating style evolved into an early parenting look with the invasion of pacifiers and pull toys? Surely your concerns and the content of your conversations have been redecorated. But of all the changes Baby has brought, none are greater than those in your heart. Share with your child the joy and meaning his life has brought yours.

Dearest Redecorator of My Heart,

Some changes in my priorities include

I find myself thinking more about

Conversations now revolve around

I'm finding such simple pleasure in

Since having you, I have changed

You have added meaning to my life by

Dear Heavenly Father,

In this season of change and new life,

....

....

Moments I want to remember from this time:

-

-

I will give you a new heart and
put a new spirit in you.

—EZEKIEL 36:26

*Babies Take Us on
a Special Journey*

Babies take us on
a special journey
into the land of love.

—SUSAN SQUELLATI FLORENCE

Oh, How He Loves

YOU

God's Plans for Your Future

photo

For this is how God loved the world:
He gave his one and only Son, so that
everyone who believes in him will not
perish but have eternal life.

—JOHN 3:16 (NLT)

Love. That one little word covers a vast array of emotions—from how we feel about our spouse to how we feel about ice cream. However, the original word used for *love* in John 3:16 is not a sugary sentiment or fleeting feeling. It is from the Greek word *agapao* and means a divine love straight from the heart of God. It is a love so strong that it required action. God agapao—loved us—so very much that He was compelled to demonstrate it. What did He do? Send flowers? Pen a poem? No, at great cost to Himself, He gave His Son so that we could experience lasting forgiveness and eternal life with Him. Now that is love in action.

Look into the eyes of your newborn. Can you even begin to imagine loving someone so much that you would sacrifice your own child for that person? Not only does God love you that much, but He also loves your baby with that active intensity. Think of the ramifications for her life! How will you show Baby God's love in action? Tell Baby what it means to you to know that God sacrificed His own child to save you and yours.

Dearest Loved One,

I first heard God loved me ....

....

....

....

My faith in God has made a difference in my life by ....

....

....

....

When I think about God giving His Son ....

....

....

....

Knowing how much God loves you makes me feel ....

....

....

....

To demonstrate my love for you, I ....

....

....

....

I plan to continue showing you God's love by ....

....

....

....

Dear Heavenly Father,

Thank You so much for Your love for us. I pray that

....

....

Moments I want to remember from this time:

•

•

God is love. Whoever lives in love lives in God,
and God in them.

—1 JOHN 4:16

If

If all the world were paper
And seas were ink so blue,
We couldn't write enough to tell
How much that God loves you.

—MARJORIE AINSBOROUGH
DECKER

Written on Your

HEART

A Special Prayer for You as You Grow

photo

Dear Heavenly Father,

....

....

....

....

....

....

....

....

Amen

Being confident of this, that he who
began a good work in you will carry
it on to completion until the day of
Christ Jesus.

—PHILIPPIANS 1:6

A Note from Dad

....

....

....

....

....

....

....

....

....

....

....

....

....

....

....

....

....

....

....

....

Start children off on the way they should go,
and even when they are old they will not turn from it.

—PROVERBS 22:6

Place Baby photo here

Place Baby photo here